DISCARD

j636.73 Green, Sara
GRE
Rottweilers

CHILDREN

CHILDREN'S ROOM

DEC 07 2010   509

FAIRPORT PUBLIC LIBRARY
1 Village Landing
Fairport, NY 14450

DOG BREEDS
Rottweilers

by Sara Green

Consultant:
Michael Leuthner, D.V.M.
Petcare Animal Hospital
Madison, Wisc.

BELLWETHER MEDIA • MINNEAPOLIS, MN

Note to Librarians, Teachers, and Parents:

Blastoff! Readers are carefully developed by literacy experts and combine standards-based content with developmentally appropriate text.

Level 1 provides the most support through repetition of high-frequency words, light text, predictable sentence patterns, and strong visual support.

Level 2 offers early readers a bit more challenge through varied simple sentences, increased text load, and less repetition of high-frequency words.

Level 3 advances early-fluent readers toward fluency through increased text and concept load, less reliance on visuals, longer sentences, and more literary language.

Level 4 builds reading stamina by providing more text per page, increased use of punctuation, greater variation in sentence patterns, and increasingly challenging vocabulary.

Level 5 encourages children to move from "learning to read" to "reading to learn" by providing even more text, varied writing styles, and less familiar topics.

Whichever book is right for your reader, Blastoff! Readers are the perfect books to build confidence and encourage a love of reading that will last a lifetime!

This edition first published in 2011 by Bellwether Media, Inc.

No part of this publication may be reproduced in whole or in part without written permission of the publisher. For information regarding permission, write to Bellwether Media, Inc., Attention: Permissions Department, 5357 Penn Avenue South, Minneapolis, MN 55419.

Library of Congress Cataloging-in-Publication Data
Green, Sara, 1964–
  Rottweilers / by Sara Green.
    p. cm. – (Blastoff! readers: Dog breeds)
  Includes bibliographical references and index.
  Summary: "Simple text and full-color photography introduce beginning readers to the characteristics of the dog breed Rottweilers. Developed by literacy experts for students in kindergarten through third grade"–Provided by publisher.
  ISBN 978-1-60014-460-8 (hardcover : alk. paper)
  1. Rottweiler dog–Juvenile literature. I. Title.
SF429.R7G74 2010
636.73–dc22
                                        2010000676

Text copyright © 2011 by Bellwether Media, Inc. BLASTOFF! READERS and associated logos are trademarks and/or registered trademarks of Bellwether Media, Inc.

Printed in the United States of America, North Mankato, MN.
080110   1162

Contents

What Are Rottweilers?	4
History of Rottweilers	8
Rottweilers Today	16
Glossary	22
To Learn More	23
Index	24

What Are Rottweilers?

Rottweilers are strong dogs with black **coats**. They are also called Rotties. The Rottweiler **breed** is a member of the **Working Group** of dogs. This group of dog breeds does work to help people. Rottweilers are medium to large in size. They are 22 to 27 inches (56 to 69 centimeters) tall. They weigh 85 to 130 pounds (39 to 59 kilograms).

Rottweilers have short, thick coats. Their coats are black with tan markings.

Rottweilers are born with long tails. Many owners like the look of short tails. A **veterinarian** can do an operation to **dock** a tail. However, many owners choose to keep Rottweiler tails long.

docked tail

History of Rottweilers

Mastiff

The **ancestors** of the Rottweiler breed were large dogs called Mastiffs. The Romans brought them to Germany almost 2,000 years ago. The Romans built a town called Rottweil. Some Mastiffs stayed in the town and worked as **herding dogs** and **draft dogs**.

In the 1200s, the butchers of Rottweil decided to breed a dog to help them work. They chose to **crossbreed** dogs that were smart, brave, and fast.

These dogs had puppies. They were the first Rottweilers. People named the breed after the town. Butchers used Rottweilers to herd cattle, guard money, and pull carts of goods to be sold.

! **fun fact**
Butchers used to tie pouches of money around Rottweilers' necks to keep the money safe from thieves.

By the late 1800s, butchers in Rottweil used the railroad to transport cattle. They used donkeys to pull carts. People stopped breeding Rottweilers. The breed almost became **extinct**.

Fortunately, some people thought Rottweilers could do different work. In the early 1900s, Rottweilers began working as police dogs in Germany. Soon the breed was popular again.

People brought Rottweilers to the United States in the 1920s. Many people thought the breed was unfriendly and tough. Rottweilers were mostly used as guard dogs.

Over time, people learned that Rottweilers can be calm and friendly. Rottweilers became popular **companion dogs**.

Rottweilers Today

Rottweilers enjoy many physical activities today. They still like to pull carts. Some Rottweilers and their owners participate in an activity called **carting**. Rottweilers pull their owners in carts with wheels. They even participate in cart races!

fun fact

The Rottweiler breed is known as the Rottweiler Metzgerhund in Germany. "Metzgerhund" means "butcher's dog" in German.

Rottweilers also herd and guard. They feel a strong loyalty to their owners. Farmers use them to herd their animals. They also use them as guard dogs. Rottweilers are one of the best breeds to guard people and property.

Rottweilers help people in other ways. Many Rottweilers are **therapy dogs**. They visit sick or elderly people who are in hospitals or nursing homes. People feel better after they pet a friendly Rottweiler.

Rottweilers are strong and smart. They are loyal pets that love to stay active. They especially enjoy spending time with friends!

Glossary

ancestors—family members who lived long ago

breed—a type of dog

carting—an activity where dogs pull people riding in carts

coats—the hair or fur of animals

companion dogs—dogs that provide friendship to people

crossbreed—to mate different dog breeds together to make a new breed

dock—to shorten the tail of a dog

draft dogs—dogs used to pull loads from one place to another

extinct—when every member of a species has died off

herding dogs—dogs that are used to make a group of animals move

therapy dogs—dogs that provide comfort to people

veterinarian—a doctor who takes care of animals

Working Group—dog breeds that do jobs to help humans

To Learn More

AT THE LIBRARY
American Kennel Club. *The Complete Dog Book for Kids*. New York, N.Y.: Howell Books, 1996.

Fiedler, Julie. *Rottweilers*. New York, N.Y.: PowerKids Press, 2006.

Gray, Susan H. *Rottweilers*. Mankato, Minn.: The Child's World, 2008.

ON THE WEB
Learning more about Rottweilers is as easy as 1, 2, 3.

1. Go to www.factsurfer.com.

2. Enter "Rottweilers" into the search box.

3. Click the "Surf" button and you will see a list of related Web sites.

With factsurfer.com, finding more information is just a click away.

Index

1200s, 10
1800s, 12
1900s, 13
1920s, 14
ancestors, 9
breed, 5, 9, 11, 12, 13, 14, 18, 19
butchers, 10, 11, 12, 18
cart pulling, 11, 12, 17
carting, 17
coats, 5, 6
companion dogs, 15
crossbreeding, 10
docking, 7
draft dogs, 9
extinction, 12
farmers, 19
Germany, 9, 13, 18
guard dogs, 11, 14, 19
height, 5
herding dogs, 9, 11, 19
loyalty, 19, 21

markings, 6
Mastiffs, 8, 9
owners, 7, 17, 19
police dogs, 13
Romans, 9
Rottweil, 9, 10
tails, 7
therapy dogs, 20
United States, 14
veterinarians, 7
weight, 5
Working Group, 5

The images in this book are reproduced through the courtesy of: Paul Cotney, front cover; Juniors Bildarchiv/Photolibrary, pp. 4-5; Juan Martinez, pp. 5 (small), 10-11, 12, 19 (small), 21; Juniors Bildarchiv, pp. 6-7; Ron Kimball/KimballStock, p. 7 (small); Patrik Mezirka, p. 8; Jon Eppard, p. 9; North Wind Picture Archives/Alamy, p. 11 (small); Art Directors & TRIP/Alamy, p. 13; Farlap/Alamy, p. 14; Horizon International Images Limited/Alamy, p. 15; John Daniels/Ardea, pp. 16-17; Dr. Tommy Caisango, p. 17 (small); Cameron Watson, pp. 18-19; Bonzami Emmanuelle, p. 20.